D

D1583241

emanuel ungaro

emanuel ungaro

Christine Orban

Thames & Hudson

Translated from the French by Emily Read

This edition first published in the United Kingdom in 1999 by
Thames & Hudson Ltd, 181A High Holborn, London WC1V 7QX

British Library Cataloguing-in-Publication Data
A catalogue record for this book is available from the British Library

ISBN 0-500-01966-5

Printed and bound in Italy

e manuel Ungaro speaks of houses rather as he does of women and goes as far as believing that a woman is comparable to a house.... To tell the truth, the idea would never have occurred to me if Ungaro had not prompted me. 'One must never just wear a dress, one must inhabit it. In the same way one should inhabit a house or apartment with one's thoughts.' Ungaro can see at once if a house is marked by artifice and superficial decoration; as with a woman, an accessory must remain an accessory.

Ungaro dresses and 'inhabits', he does not decorate or disguise. He goes straight to the essentials. It might appear incongruous, ambitious, perhaps, to speak of essentials when referring to clothes. However, it certainly does not seem so to this solitary music-lover who loves to wander in forests, tending to trees, this saturnine character who does not drown his sorrows amongst others, but seeks strength and sources of inspiration within himself, this pure heart which likes neither to pose nor talk about himself, who is wary of flatterers, and tolerates no compromise – someone who could give pause for thought to many a workaholic success-slave. He knows enough of the value of friendship not to overstretch it. He knows that having too many friends is suspect, and can become a sort of trade in sympathy and human relations.

By opening your door too wide, you risk losing in quality what you gain in quantity. Ungaro is not interested in quantity – only quality. Ungaro's theory of friendship is well summed up by the Chinese saying, 'Contract your heart', and Jean Cocteau's, 'Do not leave the chalk circle.' One friendship too many and the circle is broken. Ungaro saves his warmth and his treasures for those he loves.

Melancholy? Yes, melancholy is always present just beneath the surface, as if to remind one that glory, fame, money are nothing, mere accessories, the ransom for relentless work which is neither futile nor superficial, a ransom which is deserved but which has not changed him. Criticism, whether good or bad, does not affect him either; he sails along, not indifferent of course, but with a conviction that owes nothing to the encouragement of others.

h e was born in Aix-en-Provence in France, although only by chance as his parents had had to leave Apulia in Italy. Ungaro retains a nostalgia, a prenatal memory of the south of Italy, recaptured in the light and smells of Provence. He was at the heart of a family that was modest, but rich insofar as Cosimo, his father, passed on to Ungaro his love of music and dress-making. The truest present is, surely, to teach a person to love, to listen, to look. Cosimo and Concetta, his mother, also gave him five brothers and a sister, love and respect for others and, on Sundays, a dish of polpetti with fresh tomato sauce which nowadays he shares with friends, but still with unaffected pleasure. The recipe is jealously guarded and revealed as a condition of joining the clan. For the Ungaros, to receive friends is to give and to share. It does not matter where it is, whether a sumptuous dining room with cloud-painted ceiling, or a Mediterranean-style kitchen, the important thing is to drink together, out of acid-coloured Venetian glasses filled with a fine wine chosen and served by Ungaro himself. A privileged and unforgettable moment in which nothing is vain or artificial.

'the inside of the envelope is Laura', he says. This magnificent woman, her soul as fine as her body, is a magician of aromas and refined tastes, and her happiness depends on his. Laura, the woman who symbolizes all women for Ungaro, his dream come true, her expressed requests important to him even if not always implemented.

Ungaro listens to women and then does exactly as he pleases, because he knows that one must sometimes outpace what they want, surprise them with their own tastes.

Laura is the link, the reflection in the mirror. The discreet, modest Laura, who knew when she married Ungaro that she was also marrying his fashion house. She is very rarely seen in photographs, never after a collection. She hides. She has no need for glory or recognition, it is as though she knows that she owns the essence of this man, his love.

The essential, with the Ungaros, is in the look. An intense look which hides and dissimulates nothing, which never misunderstands people, and can still love them with their faults. You are friends, and it's for life. Some friendships grow; these are the type worthy of Ungaro's esteem.

I do not know if the look they share is one acquired by Laura from Emanuel, or whether they were alike even before they met. She is lighter and more mischievous, he more melancholic, a touch despondent even, but they share the same compassion, interest and generosity.

It would have been impossible for me to write about Ungaro without describing the woman who has conquered the man who loves women so much and yet only loves one, and through her all women....

The Ungaro woman.... God created women, and from them Ungaro has chosen his, both one and several.... And if they are different externally, all are touched by the grace of femininity, the desire to please, the boldness to attempt it, and the cheek to succeed.

Cheek? Why not? Elegance does not necessarily need to be respectable, elegant or provocative. The Ungaro woman can allow herself a lapse in taste, aware of having committed it (which makes all the difference), and then brandish it like a flag, with the blessing and complicity of the master.

The master does not like the conventional and the predictable; virtuosos are allowed to disobey, to interpret, to stray from the score, to play with ranges of colour, prints, materials, as though child prodigies of what is lightly called 'fashion', a word that condemns the art to the ephemeral and the transient, depending on the taste of the day.

but fashion is also a way of living, of behaving, of thinking. The French writer Gide said that 'there are fashions even in ways of suffering or loving.' Ungaro's fashion is closer to that definition. A garment by Ungaro is more a lifestyle than just a style. Ungaro works with music, and that can be felt: I can almost guess which designs he did while humming *Don Juan*, and which while listening, without allowing anyone else to make a sound, to *The Barber of Seville* or a Beethoven quartet – chamber music is a source of inspiration. At that moment he dares, he exceeds, he provokes and sometimes annoys.... The music which inspires him guides him, carries him away....

One does not wear Ungaro.... One enters into the spirit of Ungaro. The Ungaro woman becomes a militant, a fan, a groupie. Ungaro does not compromise in his friendships. I betray him, occasionally, and I feel as repentant as a guilty spouse, and so much influenced by him that, in any case, I re-create the style he has taught me even when wearing other clothes.

How many encounters, cases of love at first sight, is this man responsible for, thanks to his spirit which blows like a wind, a tempest around his creations? Those over-long shawls and over-light stoles were made to be thrown from one shoulder to the other, caressing with a sumptuously braided tassel the cheek of a neighbour delighted by such calculated yet careless grace; that little pearl-encrusted bag was made to lie, making its mark, on an embroidered tablecloth strewn with bread-crumbs and wine-stains. That fur cape was tailored to slide off and be picked up over and over again; as for the linings of the jackets and coats, their secret remains with those who took them off....

9

Sensuality is everywhere. The soft material of a simple jersey cries out to be stroked; a dress is cut to move, following the movements of the body, displaying and concealing them; because he loves women, he knows the limits of male forbearance, and creates a garment too beautiful to be torn off, but cunning enough to suggest careful removal.

If I was a husband, I would give my wife an account with Ungaro – I might even demand it as a clause in the marriage contract, as an eternal incitement to seduction.... I would like to see her one night as a Chinese woman from Shanghai in a slip, or adorned with the painted silks and distressed velvets in the colours of the river in which Ophelia slept.

●

'I am sensually obsessed', he declares. We had realized that. Obsessed with women to the point where he is not content simply to dress them, he wants to inhabit them, as I stressed at the beginning of this work, to immerse himself in their spirit, their bearing, in the perception that others have of them, and of course in their behaviour. He adds a small extra element, something indescribable which one could call charm, enchantment, bewitchment. His creature could be Carmen saying 'if I love you, beware'. Only nudity could rival the clothes he creates in order to ensnare.

He knows how to play with a woman's body, to expose it, a little, subtly implying what is there, to cover it up all the better to display it. A collection is conceived rather like a novel; the same difficulties must be surmounted, the same perhaps subconscious perseverance is necessary; one must have a general idea before drawing the first line, the first sketch. Each time Ungaro is telling a story. And like a sculptor faced with a waiting block of granite, or a painter faced with his palette, Ungaro examines the rolls of material unfolded before his house models who parade in white smocks in the studio. He crumples a striped print, wraps it over one of these sculptural women who surround him, waits, backs away, comes forward, starts again.... Ungaro likes to be on his own ground. Of course he dreams up his collection in the woods, in the streets, in the bath maybe..., but he also needs to touch solid matter, to feel the heat of flesh, and the softness of a woman's skin in order to construct his melody. The name of the garment, whether skirt or trousers, does not matter, what is important is its function, its purpose. Ungaro loves freedom above all, and allows for an incredible range of possibilities for combining his clothes. Thus each woman can be creative in turn, adjusting the clothes to her own temperament, or to the mood of the day, making them unique. One has to appropriate the garment, adding one's imprint to Ungaro's, like an act of love; the material, the tissue itself is him, the man enveloping the body, covering it, caressing it in order to redraw a new or renewed woman, newly born or born again.

Ungaro has re-created so many types of women.... The diva, her body sculpted in pleated white silk, the prized Greek statue, suddenly enlivening the shows; the oriental beauty draped in a thousand veils, with printed trousers; the 'chic hippy' in symbolist-inspired browns and golds; the Parisienne in a perfect suit, with an innovative mixture of colours; the gypsy, a memory of his childhood in Aix-en-Provence, the long wandering silhouette, relaxed in a printed skirt and a striped man's jacket; I will always remember her, a good luck charm symbolizing fidelity to the past. The gypsy is there in all the shows, like a guardian angel that has never abandoned him. She appears on the podium to those who can recognize her, she finds a place whatever story Ungaro is telling, because his collections are outside time and cannot go out of fashion.

There have always been divas and gypsies, urchins and tarts. And what woman has not dreamt of being one or other, or one and other? Ungaro knows how to play with women's whims, how to transform a diaphanous vamp into a tomboy, with straight trousers and impeccable turn-ups, with a high waist, a fob-watch if necessary, a shirt, a morning-coat ... why not? The trousers could as well be grey cloth as white, gold or navy blue lace, letting one see the curve of the leg, the grace of the knees, and, depending on the length of the jacket, the slenderness of the thighs....

Ungaro likes swan necks and his collars can be very high to emphasize them; his complicity with women makes him realize that one can reveal more by concealment, that one can, with a multitude of finely sewn little buttons down the back or on the wrist, surmount many small difficulties and render a woman both desirable and inaccessible. Seduction cannot be taken for granted. None of this can be understood by someone who has never worn a dress by Emanuel Ungaro.

What does a woman want? If Freud was unable to answer that question, I certainly wouldn't have the pretension to offer a solution. Neither would Ungaro, even though he has spent his life pondering the question and attempting to offer some enlightenment. Women wish to please, and to please men in particular....

Of course there are different ways of doing this: intelligence, talent, something indefinable in the look, the skin, a way of crossing the legs, all more in God's domain than in that of the couturier – I almost said 'creator'. And evidently the word has a significance outside the language of fashion. Ungaro offers the look, but also the message – there is always a message implicit in what one has chosen to wear. Ungaro's shapes, colours and materials are every bit as eloquent as words.

ince Ungaro loves women, he addresses himself to men, just as some other designers create for women by becoming so close to them that they identify themselves with them. Ungaro's approach is the opposite. He dresses them for himself, and for them, his fellow men. He dresses women almost egoistically. He adorns them because he desires them. This explains the evident sensuality which emanates from all his clothes. A woman will love a dress that draws the attention of a man she is attracted to, and to that extent he answers Sigmund Freud's question.

I do not know any man used to the company of a woman dressed by Ungaro who regrets the day she changed her style. I have overheard conversations between men, who were neither frivolous nor effeminate, in which they spoke of their pride and pleasure in recognizing and looking at a woman dressed by Ungaro.

His clothes have been described as erotic and sensual.... One wants to avoid the word 'fashion' with him. Chanel maintained that 'fashion is something that goes out of fashion'; a fine and modest remark, but I am sure that it does justice neither to her nor to Ungaro.

Creating a collection is not an ephemeral action when the creation is part of a style, an architecture, a rigorous spirit. Ungaro's philosophy comes from his master, just as other masters have masters.... What would Mozart be without Haydn, Ungaro without Cristobal Balenciaga, master of the future master who in 1958 took him on as his assistant in his studio in Paris. 'A good designer must be an architect for the plans, a sculptor for the form, a painter for the colour, a musician for the harmony, and a philosopher as well.' Message understood. But since nothing grows in the shade of great trees, after six years with Balenciaga, Ungaro, already trained at cutting very young by his father, sold his car and left, with a little money in his pocket and a few influences which he would shed, and went to avenue MacMahon with his friend Sonia Knapp to embark on the great adventure.

a s I began this book by comparing a woman to a house, I will pursue the metaphor: only the strongest architecture can support eccentricity; only someone with talent can take risks. Risk becomes a marker. In the United States elegant women make no mistakes, and for them the unclassifiable Ungaro symbolizes refinement, real French chic.

Ungaro was not made to stay still, even as the head of a fashion house. He had to continue to climb, to impart what is within him, for the happiness of others, to leave behind his beloved parents and home-land, but always knowing deep inside himself that his parents and Aix-en-Provence will remain with him. Ungaro remains faithful to himself. No life can be lived without some pain. He is all the more faithful to his roots in the knowledge that the fruits of his success have enabled him to return to his native land and buy a magical property. He does not spend much time at this house, but it is there, and the thought of it is enough to reassure him.

Suffering? Could suffering be the source of that dazzling range of shapes and colours?

He did not choose to use suffering as his driving force; the saddest, most passionate love story can become a journey of initiation.

At fifteen, Ungaro used to make himself seriously ill. Months in bed gave him the opportunity to reflect on his dreamlike relationship with women, and this was the origin of his vocation: 'I set off into the realm of dream, desire, longing, in a way which is sometimes frightening.'

Ungaro never spares his own feelings in his work. Beyond know-how and academicism, a garment is nothing if it is not transcended by emotion, the most difficult thing to impart. Emotion as primary matter. If this exercise was to find a single word to sum up the work of Ungaro, that is the one I would choose. According to Paul Claudel, 'poetry cannot exist without emotion', neither can Ungaro's design. Look at his clothes, touch them: one can almost hear the melody and feel the breath of the creator in each of them. These pretty things conceal tormented passion, but with delicacy and modesty.

Chronology

1933   13 February, Emanuel Ungaro is born in Aix-en-Provence, France. His father and mother, Cosimo Damiano and Concetta Casalino, Italians who were originally from Apulia, had emigrated to France. Emanuel is the second of seven children.

1950   In the early fifties, after an apprenticeship with a tailor in Aix-en-Provence, he works as a trainee in his father's workshop.

1956   Arrives in Paris and joins Camps, men's tailors. Has a group of friends, all from the South of France: the stylist Jean Barthet, the sculptor César, and Yves Klein; gets to know photographer Peter Knapp.

1958   Joins Cristobal Balenciaga, the couturier, at avenue George V, Paris.

1960   Becomes director of the Balenciaga studio in Madrid. He dresses, amongst others, the Spanish royal family and the duchess of Alba.

1961   Returns to Balenciaga in Paris.

1965   With the help of a few workers, he opens his own house in avenue MacMahon, Paris, and organizes two shows a year. His early clients include Mrs Onassis, Mrs Niarchos, Mme Bettencourt and Marie-Hélène de Rothschild.

1967   Opens showroom at 2 avenue Montaigne, Paris.

1968   Opens the first Emanuel Ungaro ready-to-wear boutique, on the ground floor of the showroom.

1969   Receives the Neiman Marcus Award in Texas.

1970   Ungaro Parallèle is distributed in the American department stores Bonwit Teller, Neiman Marcus and I. Magnin.

1971   Ungaro Parallèle distributed in Japan. Receives Best Designer award in Mexico and the Rouet d'or prize in Krefeld, Germany.

1973   Launches men's collection, 'Ungaro Uomo'.

1974   Opens Emanuel Ungaro Homme at 2 avenue Montaigne, Paris.

1975   Dresses Catherine Deneuve in Jean-Paul Rappeneau's film, *Le Sauvage*. Second Emanuel Ungaro boutique opens in rue du Faubourg-St-Honoré, Paris.

1977   First exclusive Emanuel Ungaro boutique opens in New York.

1978   Creates 'Ungaro TER' line for Europe.

1979   Dresses Gena Rowlands in John Cassavetes' film *Gloria*.

1980   Receives French couture's Golden Dice award.

Linda Evangelista in a flowery puff-ball dress (1987)
© Photo Bill King/French Vogue 1987

1981   In Japan, *Women's Wear Daily* places him amongst their top five designers.
Dresses Isabelle Huppert in Joseph Losey's *la Truite*.

1982   Creates 'Ungaro Solo Donna' line for Europe.
Dresses Isabelle Adjani in Claude Miller's *Mortelle Randonnée* (Fatal Journey).

1983   Launch of Diva, a perfume for women.
In January, meets the actress Anouk Aimée, for whom he designs the costumes for Claude Lelouch's *Viva la vie*. She continues to embody the Ungaro image in publicity campaigns for his ready-to-wear collections until 1987.

1984   Ungaro showroom opens in Milan, Italy.
Dresses Anouk Aimée in Jerzy Skolimowski's *Success is the Best Revenge*.

1985   Launch of Ungaro Inc. in New York.

1986   Creates 'Solo Donna' and 'Ungaro TER' for the United States.
Designs Anouk Aimée's costumes for Claude Lelouch's *Vingt ans déjà*.

1987   Nominated for the fashion oscars in Paris.
Launch of 'Senso', a perfume for women, and the 'Mer et Bateau' line.

1989   Marries the Italian Laura Bernabei.

1990   Birth of his daughter Cosima.
Launch of 'Ungaro', a perfume for women.
Wins Mod Woche prize in Munich, Germany.

1991   Launches the men's fragrance 'Ungaro' and the 'Emanuel/Emanuel Ungaro' line in New York.
Awarded Ville de Marseille prize.

1992   On the twenty-fifth anniversary of the fashion house, the book *Ungaro* is published by Editions Electa in collaboration with the GFT (Gruppo Finanziario Tessile, the manufacturers of Ungaro ready-to-wear collections).
Launch of the men's fragrance 'Ungaro pour l'Homme II' and the new version of the women's perfume 'Senso'.

1993   Launch of the men's fragrance 'Ungaro pour l'Homme III'.

1995   University of Shanghai makes him honorary professor.

1996   Beginning of association with the Salvatore Ferragamo trademark.
Launch of 'Emanuel Ungaro U Collection' and 'Emanuel Ungaro Knitwear'.

1997   Dresses Marisa Berenson in Bunny Schpoliansky's *Belles, riches, etc.*
Joins Salvatore Ferragamo and Bulgari to create a company: Emanuel Ungaro Parfums.
Launch of 'Emanuel/Emanuel Ungaro Liberté' and the 'Week-End' line in New York.

1998   Dresses Sharon Stone in the European publicity campaign for Martini & Rossi, and designs thirty dresses for her in Albert Brooks' film *The Muse*.
Launch of 'Chaussures et Sacs Emanuel Ungaro', made by Salvatore Ferragamo.

1999   Launch of 'Lunettes Homme et Femme' in collaboration with Luxottica.

'Cowgirl' style (1970)
© Photo Peter Knapp

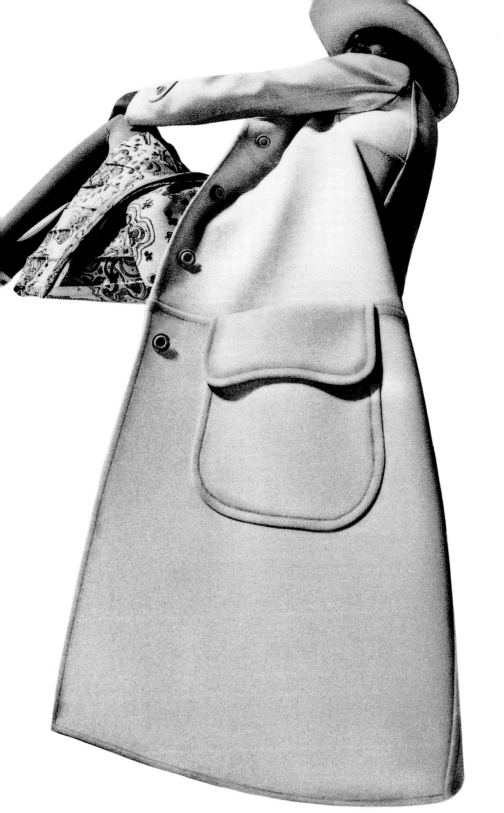

Emanuel Ungaro

Quest for a new technology to make a long coat (1969). © Photo Peter Knapp.
Discovery of coloured stripes (1969). Materials: Sonja Knapp. © Photo Peter Knapp.

Checks and stripes (1973). © Photo Peter Knapp.
Geometric aesthetics. Short dress and striped coat in wool (1966). © Photo Peter Knapp.

'Russian folk' style: seamless coats over scarf-skirts made of wool chenille fabric and printed silk (1976). © Photo Duane Michaels/French *Vogue* 1976.

Sobriety. Two striped coats with fur collars (1973). © Photo Peter Knapp.
Early flower prints (late sixties). © Photo Peter Knapp.

Dream of perfection (1980). © Photo Daniel Jouanneau.
Sixties geometry. Trapeze dress of double thickness coat material (1965). © Photo Fouli Elia/Elle/Scoop.

Pleated bustier dresses. Spot-printed dresses decorated with flowers, a favourite accessory of Ungaro (1984). Photo Harris Gaffin. © All Rights Reserved/ Ungaro Archives.
One colour surprise. Bustier dress with pink satin bow (1992). © Photo Albert Watson.

Two styles from the ready-to-wear collection spring/summer 1979. © Photo
François Lamy.
Iman modelling a spotted draped dress (1988). © Photo Tyen.

Spots on a palette of primary colours. Finale of the ready-to-wear collection
show spring/summer 1985. © Photo Patrice Stable/Ungaro Archives.

A mixture of materials; a mixture of themes. Silk and wool chiffon; spots,
stripes and checks (1985). © Photo Arthur Elgort.
Anouk Aimée: a new sensual image for a powerful woman from the ready-to-
wear collection spring/summer 1986. Photo Guy Bourdin. © Samuel Bourdin.

Encounter with Deborah Turbeville. Feminine opulence in a decadent atmos-
phere from the couture collection autumn/winter 1986–1987. © Photo
Deborah Turbeville.

Silky textures. Finale of a ready-to-wear collection show (mid-eighties). © All
Rights Reserved/Ungaro Archives.

Inspired by the sculpture of César (1991). Each year, the entire workshop
traditionally applauds the wedding dress. © Photo Roxanne Lowit.

Marisa Berenson: ode to sensuality in a purple ball dress (1995). © Photo Jean-Marie Perrier/*Elle*/Scoop.
End of the evening on the Pont Alexandre III in Paris (1995). © Photo Walter Chin.

Emanuel Ungaro's black swan (1991). © Italian *Vogue* Archives.
Sharon Stone at the film preview of *101 Dalmatians*. Dazzling in an Ungaro dress embroidered with ostrich feathers (1996). © All Rights Reserved/Ungaro Archives.

Passionate red for Anouk Aimée (1986). Photo Guy Bourdin. © Samuel Bourdin.

The Ungaro universe seen by Deborah Turbeville from the couture collection autumn/winter 1986–1987. © Photo Deborah Turbeville.

Draped dress in panther print (1997). © Photo Peter Lindbergh.
Feminine/masculine (1997). © Photo Christophe Kutner.

The couturier's dream (1995). © Photo Jean-Marie Perrier/*Elle*/Scoop.

Country folk style. © Photo Peter Knapp.
Gypsy-inspired pleated skirt and Scottish tartan shawl, lined with Ikat (1992). © Photo Walter Chin.

The new Eve (1998). © Photo Michael Thompson/French *Vogue* 1998.

The violence of flowers in the intimacy of a boudoir. Anouk Aimée by Guy Bourdin (1986). © Samuel Bourdin.

The softness of a flowered print. Renata Maciel Dos Santos modelling for the publicity campaign for the ready-to-wear collection spring/summer 1999. (Courtesy Next Models) Courtesy Italian *Vogue*. © Photo Regan Cameron.

The fragility of lace from the couture collection autumn/winter 1998–1999. Courtesy Italian *Vogue*. © Photo Regan Cameron.
A fairy in a wood from the couture collection autumn/winter 1998–1999. Courtesy Italian *Vogue*. © Photo Regan Cameron.

The heat of a hammam from the publicity campaign for the ready-to-wear collection spring/summer 1998. © Photo Martin Thompson.
Provocation: a sensuous lingerie ensemble from the publicity campaign for the ready-to-wear collection spring/summer 1999. Courtesy Italian *Vogue*. © Photo Regan Cameron.

Christine Orban: interpreter of the Ungaro style and great friend of the designer. Photo Bettina Rheims. © Christine Orban.
The twenties re-visited from the ready-to-wear collection autumn/winter 1993–1994. © Photo Arthur Elgort.

An Italian Renaissance prince? Interpretation of a painting by Bronzino (1988). © Photo Mario Testino.

End of evening in the medina: softness of light and colour of prints from the couture collection spring/summer 1999. Courtesy Italian *Vogue*. © Photos Regan Cameron.

Emanuel Ungaro by Jeanloup Sieff. © Photo Jeanloup Sieff.
The studio. © Photo Frédérick Andrieu.

The publishers would like to thank the Emanuel Ungaro fashion house: Laura Ungaro, Gianbattista Valli, Alessia Margiotta-Broglio, and particularly Capucine Safyurtlu and Isabelle Konikoff, for their assistance in preparing this book.

Thanks are also due to Anouk Aimée, Marisa Berenson, Linda Evangelista (Elite), Iman, Teresa Lourenco (Women), Renata Maciel Dos Santos (Next Models), Sharon Stone, Frédérick Andrieu, Regan Cameron, Walter Chin, Arthur Elgort, Fouli Elia, Harris Gaffin, Daniel Jouanneau, Bill King, Peter Knapp, Christophe Kutner, François Lamy, Peter Lindbergh, Roxanne Lowit, Duane Michaels, Jean-Marie Perrier, Jeanloup Sieff, Patrice Stable, Mario Testino, Martin Thompson, Michael Thompson, Deborah Turbeville, Tyen and Albert Watson.

Finally, this work would not have been possible without the kind assistance of Alexandre (Elite), Samuel Bourdin, Cordelia (Select), Edouard and Sandrine (Filomeno), Eric (Serlin & Townsend), Chris Fioto (Marek & Associates), Chantal Goupil (WWD), Diane Heidkruger (Elite), Katie (Jet Root), Claudine Legros (*Elle*/Scoop), Félix N'Yeurt, Marina Rossi (Italian *Vogue*), Sandrine (Tyen), Jessica Sarres (Albert Watson, Inc.) and Brigitte Sondag (Art & Partner).